Life Stories of 'Allamah Sayyid 'Alī Qāḍī Ṭabāṭabā'ī

I0518052

AL-BURĀQ

Copyright

ISBN: 978-1-956276-35-0
Printed and published by al-Burāq Publications.
Translated and annotated by al-Burāq Publications.
Context and transliterations added as needed. Some minor edits were made to the translated Farsi text.

www.al-Buraq.org
publications@al-Buraq.org

First Edition | March 2023

Dedication

The publication of this book was made possible through the generous support of our donors.

بسم الله الرحمن الرحيم
الحمد لله رب العالمين الرحمن الرحيم
مالك يوم الدين إياك نعبد وإياك نستعين
اهدنا الصراط المستقيم صراط الذين
أنعمت عليهم غير المغضوب عليهم
ولا الضالين

Please recite *Sūrat al-Fātihah* and ask God for the Divine reward (*thawāb*) to be conferred upon the donors and also the souls of all the deceased in whose memory their loved ones have contributed graciously towards the publication of *Life Stories of ʿAllamah Sayyid ʿAlī Qāḍī Ṭabāṭabāʾī.*

We begin by giving all praise and thanks to God ﷻ for giving us the *tawfīq* to translate this book. He has guided us and without Him, we would not have been guided to the straight path embodied by the Prophet Muḥammad ﷺ and the Ahl al-Bayt عليهم السلام.

This book is dedicated to all the scholars, martyrs and believers who worked tirelessly to promote the pure Muḥammadan path.

We want to also give our thanks and appreciation to all believers from around the world and acknowledge the team which helped al-Burāq Publications complete this work, spending countless hours to make its publication possible. Please recite *Sūrat al-Fātiḥah* on behalf of them, their families, and their marḥūmīn.

This book is dedicated in honor of the following individuals. Please remember them in your prayers and may God ﷻ have mercy on them and their loved ones.

Akber Hussain

Ali Ftouni

Ali Rafidhi

Aliraza Ghasemi

All Marhumeens

Alya Agemy

Amirali J. Datoo

Asiya Jafri

Bande Khuda

Baqar Jafri

Baqir Datoo

Basheerunnisa Begum

Chuweid Al Mosherafawi

Fatima Kaneez

Fatmabai P. Walji

Ghulam Hasnain

Gulam Sherali

Haaj Ali M. Shirazi

Haj Mohsan Srour

Hajj Abdulhamid Elsaghir

Hajj Abdulkarim Elsaghir

Hajj Ahmad Sheet

Hajj Fatima Nahle

Hajj Hassan Sobh

Hajj Khoudor Daher

Hajj Sami Ftouni

Hajji Amneh Sobh-Ftouni

Hajji Hiam Hojeije

Hajji Iman Elsaghir

Hajji Imane Srour

Hajji Raoufi Sheet

Hajji Sikneh Hamka

Hajji Zahya Fawaz

Hamid Jafri

Hassan Jafri

Humayun Ali Baig

Husain Jafri

Hydri B. M. Moosavi

Kemal Yilmaz

Khatija Jafri

Kulsoom Jafri

Leila Mansour

Marazia Nassarali Merali (Datoo)

Mazahir Jafri

Mehrunissa Shariff (Gadagwala)

Miqdad A. Datoo

Mohammad Baghdadi

Mohammed H. Jafri

Mujtaba H. Jafri

Munnawar Jehan

Nafees Khan

Qumber Bhimji

Rai Railey

Sabiha N. H. Jafri

Sajjad Hasnie

Saleem Thariani

Salman Al Mosherafawi

Sayyid Edris M. A. Saleh

Sayyid Hajj Khaled M. A. Saleh

Sayyid Sobh H. Sobh

Shahīd Ibrahim Hadi

Shahīd Imad Balout

Shandar Fatima

Syed A. Moosavi

Syed Askari H. Moosavi

Syed Farrukh H. Zaidi

Syed Mehdi H. Rizvi

Syed Nawab R. Kazmi

Syed Nurul H. Jafri

Syeda Siraj Fatima

Turfah Sobh

Zohra Husain

Duʿāʾ al-Ḥujjah

اللَّهُمَّ كُنْ لِوَلِيِّكَ الْحُجَّةِ بْنِ الْحَسَنِ صَلَوَاتُكَ
عَلَيْهِ وَعَلَى آبَائِهِ فِي هَذِهِ السَّاعَةِ وَفِي كُلِّ
سَاعَةٍ وَلِيّاً وَحَافِظاً وَقَائِداً وَنَاصِراً وَدَلِيلاً
وَعَيْناً حَتَّى تُسْكِنَهُ أَرْضَكَ طَوْعاً وَتُمَتِّعَهُ فِيهَا طَوِيلاً

O God, be, for Your representative, the Ḥujjat (proof), son of al-Ḥasan, Your blessings be upon him and his forefathers, in this hour and in every hour: a guardian, a protector, a leader, a helper, a proof, and an eye - until You make him live on the Earth, in obedience (to You), and cause him to live in it for a long time.

Terms of Respect

The following Arabic phrases have been used throughout this book in their respective places to show the reverence which the noble personalities deserve.

عزّ وجلّ

Used for God, meaning:
Exalted and Sublime (Perfect) is He

صلى الله عليه وآله

Used for Prophet Muḥammad, meaning:
Blessings from God be upon him and his family

عليه السلام

Used for a man (singular) of a high status, meaning:
Peace be upon him

عليها السلام

Used for a woman (singular) of a high status, meaning:
Peace be upon her

عليهما السلام

Used for men/women (dual) of a high status, meaning:
Peace be upon them both

عليهم السلام

Used for men and/or women (plural) of a high status, meaning:
Peace be upon them all

عجّل الله تعالى فرجه الشريف

Used for Imām Muḥammad al-Mahdī, meaning:
May God hasten his return

قدّس سرّه

Used for a deceased scholar, meaning:
May his resting [burial] place remain pure

Transliteration Table

The method of transliteration of Islamic terminology from the Arabic language has been carried out according to the standard transliteration table below.

ء	ʾ	ر	r	ف	f
ا	a	ز	z	ق	q
ب	b	س	s	ك	k
ت	t	ش	sh	ل	l
ث	th	ص	ṣ	م	m
ج	j	ض	ḍ	ن	n
ح	ḥ	ط	ṭ	و	w
خ	kh	ظ	ẓ	ه	h
د	d	ع	ʿ	ي	y
ذ	dh	غ	gh		
		Long Vowels			
ا	ā	و	ū	ي	ī
		Short Vowels			
ـَ	a	ـُ	u	ـِ	i

Table of Contents

Preamble

بسم الله الرحمن الرحيم

In the Name of God, the Beneficent, the Merciful

Like any other revolution, the Islamic Revolution of Iran was based upon specific objectives and ideals. One of those objectives, which the current Supreme Leader, Sayyid ʿAlī Ḥusaynī Khāminaʾī, identifies as being one of the 'greatest hopes of the Revolution' and one that is 'usually not paid sufficient attention to', is the 'creation of an environment that allows for spiritual growth and for the chains of lust and anger to be broken by all those who are prepared to do so.'[1]

As the movement towards any ideal requires a blueprint, what is the blueprint for the ideal mentioned above? The Supreme Leader, in this regard, points towards one specific blueprint that encapsulates all strata of society, be it the scholars, youth, or the general public. He terms

---

1 A statement made to a group of students on May 28th, 2018.

this blueprint the "mystical order of Āyatullāh Qāḍī."[2]

Unfortunately, this order ought to be recognized in the way and manner that it ought to be. Who was he? What was his state and condition? How did he live? These and other questions still need to be answered for many.

As such, we decided to take it upon ourselves to collect and analyze the anecdotes, stories, and statements that have been made concerning this great Islamic mystic. Using this effort, we could remove our portion of the burden carried on our beloved leader's shoulders. A leader who desires the youth of the Islamic Ummah, the commanders of the soft war, to follow in the footsteps of the likes of Sayyid 'Alī Qāḍī and to climb the ladder of spirituality, wayfaring, and to reach ultimate felicity. The youth should use

[2] Statements made to the committee responsible for holding the honoring ceremony of Āyatullāh Sayyid 'Alī Qāḍī ؒ on July 16th, 2012. This order began with Sayyid 'Alī Shushtarī ؒ, it was continued by Shaykh Mullā Ḥusayn Qulī Hamadanī ؒ, then Sayyid Aḥmad Karbalā'ī ؒ, then his student Sayyid 'Alī Qāḍī. It then reached the students of Sayyid Qāḍī, in particular 'Allāmah Muḥammad Ḥusayn Ṭabātabā'ī ؒ.

this opportunity that the Islamic Revolution has created for them and, amid all the noise and corruption surrounding them, aim to reach those heights per their capacity and capability.

This present book is a small sample of the spiritual states and sayings of Sayyid ʿAlī Qāḍī that aims to portray a mere example of his unique personality.

Dear reader, know that according to numerous proofs and confirmations, the warm, welcoming existence of Sayyid ʿAlī Qāḍī did not come to an end with his worldly passing. It may be that, through his words and stories in this book, you feel the spiritual breath and loving embrace of this illuminated teacher in your life, God-willing.

The Teacher

Story 1: Flowing Tears

"Congratulations on your newborn baby boy!"

Tears of joy started to flow from the father's eyes. Taking the newborn into his arms, his mind started wondering about the past. How long he had desired for God to grant him a son. He remembered the day he visited the Doyen of the Martyrs shrine, Imām al-Ḥusayn عليه السلام, and made that vow.

On the 13th of Dhū al-Ḥijjah 1285 AH[3], the favor of Imām al-Ḥusayn عليه السلام manifested itself.

He was named Sayyid ʿAlī.

Story 2: The Young *Mujtahid*

From the beginning of his youth, Sayyid ʿAlī occupied himself with studies. He learned Arabic and Persian grammar, Qurʾānic exegesis, jurisprudence, principles of jurisprudence, and so on from some of the most well-known teachers in Tabrīz.

---

[3] March 27th, 1869.

During these early days, he wrote his glosses on the book '*al-Irshād*' of Shaykh Mufīḍ.

However, there was a thirst within him that was not quenched through this knowledge.

It was then, at the age of 23, that he made his way to the city of Najaf, 'Irāq. It was here, at the tender age of 27, that he reached the level of *ijtihād*[4].

Story 3: The Starting Point

During the period of performing *ziyāra*, his state would change drastically. He would lose his tranquility and peace, walking to Karbalā' and back. Such a state is not unexpected from a person who would constantly say, "Whatever I have is from the Master of the Martyrs and the Noble Qur'ān. A person cannot reach the station of true monotheism from any path other than that of Imām al-Ḥusayn ﷺ."

[4] That is, he reached the level of being able to derive Islamic laws from authentic Islamic sources. (Translator's Note)

Story 4: The Invite

Whilc walking towards the prayer gathering of one of his friends, he suddenly stopped and returned home. He had noticed that the invite was not for the sake of God ﷻ but for the organizers to boast and say, "Qāḍī has come to our gathering".

Story 5: The Eyes

For close to twenty years, he was wary about his eyes, less their gaze fell upon a *non-maḥram*[5] lady.

As a result, his eyes made it a habit that whenever a non-maḥram desired to enter them, they would close shut.

Story 6: State of Poverty

He tried to attain his daily sustenance, but his condition was such that only a little of his material wealth remained. He did not complain;

[5] Generally, a non-maḥram lady is any lady with whom marriage is allowed. (Translator's Note)

he saw this state of destituteness as a favor from God ﷻ and a means towards perfection.

Sometimes, some would reproach him, saying, "How can you afford to look after such a large family?" He would answer them meticulously, "I prefer this state. In the face of the Absolute Needless, I must be the neediest. When I have no money, I feel a greater need for God and am more attentive toward Him. In this state, I think, "Will this pleasure that I take from prayer also transpire in purgatory (*Barzakh*)?"

He often said, "My 'purgatory' is poverty in this material world. Hence, I should have no issues in purgatory."

Story 7: Repercussions

Once during his youth, he was walking through the bazaar of Najaf with Sayyid Abū Ḥasan Iṣfahānī ؒ. They were close friends and discussion partners. While walking, Sayyid ʿAlī turned to Sayyid Abū Ḥasan and said, "The future of the religious authority belongs to you!' He jokingly said, "At that time, do not forget about us!"

He told one of his students many years later, "During my youth, I made a heedless joke that until today, I feel the repercussions of those baseless words."

Story 8: Always Being in the State of Ablution

There was never a time when he would awake from sleep and not return to bed without being in ablution. He would always say, 'For twenty years, I have always been in ablution. During that same time, I have not slept except in ablution.'

Story 9: The Lettuce

One day, as I entered the greengrocer, I noticed that Sayyid Qāḍī was kneeling, examining bunches of lettuce. However, surprisingly, he was only picking up those which were decaying and going dry. He paid the store owner for his items, placed them under his cloak, and went. I went after him. On reaching him, I said, "Sayyid, I have a question. Why were you examining the old and going off lettuce? People usually avoid them."

He responded, "My dear brother, this seller is a poor and impoverished man. On occasion I try to assist him, however, I prefer to give him something in exchange for something else, lest his honor and dignity get ruined or, God forbid, he makes getting things for free a habit and begins to slack in acquiring his sustenance. I knew that these lettuce bunches would never have been purchased by anyone and would have been thrown out by the owner when he closed his shop for the afternoon. It makes no difference to us whether we eat crisp, fresh lettuce or these!"

Story 10: Please Correct My Mistakes

I used to reside on the first floor of the Hindī School in Najaf. I would constantly notice that a group of students would gather in the southern section to listen to the talks of an Iranian sayyid. They would all speak in either Turkish or Persian.

While I was taking ablution one day, Sayyid came to the fountain. As was my habit, I began reciting the supplication for taking ablution. Just as I finished reciting the first section of the supplication, the Sayyid turned towards me and corrected my recitation. I became infuriated. He was Iranian, and I was a native Arab who knew the language fluently. Arrogance took hold of my existence. I told myself, "I need to teach this Sayyid a proper lesson!' I began to argue and defend my recitation in any way I could. He waited till I finished speaking. As soon as I finished, with great poise, he began to speak with me in classical Arabic. I became astounded. For a moment, I saw a scholar well-learned in an academic discussion's intricacies. Inadvertently I said to him, "Do you permit me to attend your classes?"

He nodded in approval and said, "I will speak to you in Arabic, so promise me that if I make any mistakes in my speech, you will correct them."

Story 11: Forty Thousand Words

He was well-versed in the rules and art of reciting the Noble Qur'ān (*tajwīd).* Because of this, very few reciters of the Noble Qur'ān dared to recite in his presence.

He was unmatched in his knowledge of Arabic. He had forty thousand words memorized. He would recite Arab poetry in such a manner that even the Arabs could not tell that he was Iranian.

One day, one of the scholars said, "I have such a command over Arabic grammar and poetry that if a non-Arab were to recite a poem in Arabic, I would be able to tell that the reciter was a non-Arab; even if that poem contained the highest levels of eloquence and rhetoric."

Just then, Sayyid Qāḍī began to recite an Arabic poem and, while reciting it, inserted a few couplets from himself within it. After finishing, he asked the scholar, "Which of these stanzas were from a non-Arab?" The scholar remained silent.

Story 12: Duty

While I was in Najaf, I went to visit Sayyid Qāḍī. On seeing me, he said, "Your father and I were very close friends. We would bring each other food and do the other's laundry. I still acknowledge that duty upon my shoulders. So, as long as you are in Najaf, your lunch is on me."

I did not take his offer very seriously, and the day passed. The next day, to my surprise, I saw Sayyid Qāḍī at lunchtime holding a piece of flatbread and a bowl of meat stew. Then, I realized he was serious about what he had said the day before. However, his offer did not end there. He said, "If you have any laundry, please give it to me." I thought I could not make him do my laundry; the lunch was more than enough. While I was thinking, one of his students came to me and whispered, "Even if it is just a small piece of clothing, give it to him. Otherwise, he will become distraught."Reluctantly, I also had to give him my dirty clothes! This continued for my entire stay in Najaf.

Story 13: For Imām al-Ḥusayn ﷺ

His home would be the venue for the weekly remembrance gathering of Imām al-Ḥusayn ﷺ. He would say, "I have to do something for Imām al-Ḥusayn ﷺ, whether I be illiterate or a scholar."

The name of Imām al-Ḥusayn عليه السلام would cause him to become uneasy. Whenever the blessed name of the Imām عليه السلام was mentioned, he would begin to cry.

It was sufficient for the speaker to begin his talk by sending salutations to the Imām for the tears to start flowing from his eyes. This would continue till the end of the speech.

He would always say, "The flow of God's grace and blessings passes through the path of the Master of Martyrs. Moreover, the one charged with the virtue [of delivering this grace] is the Moon of the Banū Hāshim, Abū al-Faḍl al-ʿAbbās."

Story 14: Passport Issue

One of the traders of Najaf traveled to Mashhad to perform the ziyāra of Imām ʿAlī al-Riḍā عليه السلام. When he wanted to return, he found some issues with his passport. He became perplexed and did not know what to do in this city where he was a stranger.

One day, out of nowhere, he sees Sayyid Qāḍī in the mausoleum of Imām 'Alī al-Riḍā ﷺ. Hastily, he goes up to him and explains the situation. Sayyid Qāḍī says to him, "Go to the police station tomorrow; your issue will be resolved." The next day, when he went to the police station, his issue was resolved miraculously.

On his return to Najaf, he described these events to his friends. To his astonishment, they all replied, "But we saw Sayyid Qāḍī walking the streets of Najaf during those days. He did not travel anywhere."

The trader then told this story to Sayyid Qāḍī himself. "I was in Najaf. Everyone knows that during these days I did not travel." was the answer he received.

This story reached the ears of some of the seminary students. Inquisitively, they went to the Sayyid and asked him about this story, but the Sayyid merely repeated the same answer he gave to the trader.

Before this event, Sayyid Qāḍī was not very known and recognized. However, with the disclosure of this event, some of the scholars and students of Najaf requested him on numerous occasions to begin a class on ethics for them. With the start of these classes, the door for others to become acquainted with him was slowly opened.

Story 15: Absolute Need

"I have nothing." My teacher heard this statement till the end of his life. He would sign his poetry with the pseudonym *'miskīn'* (the impoverished one).

When he walks with his students, he walks behind them. No matter how much his students would insist, "Sayyid, please walk in front of us." Once he said to one of his students, "God knows that I am not the person you think I am. I am no different from you. Who knows? Maybe Jāsim, the janitor,[6] will pass through the Day of Judgment without any hindrance, while

[6] This is a way of saying that even a lowlife or uneducated person.

I will remain on the plain of the Hereafter for a lengthy time."

Story 16: Ask for God's Love God

He would advise his students to read the following supplication in the *qunūt* of their compulsory and supererogatory prayers:

اللّهُمَّ ارزُقنی حُبَّکَ وَ حُبَّ ما تُحِبُّهُ وَحُبَّ مَن یُحِبُّکَ وَ
العَمَلَ الَّذی یُبَلِّغُنی اِلی حُبِّکَ وَ اجعَل حُبَّکَ اَحَبَّ
الأَشیاءِ اِلَیَّ

"O God! Grant me Your love, and the love of that which You love, and the love of those who love You. And make me love those acts that will enable me to reach your love. And place Your love as the most special thing to me."

Story 17: Another Fish, Please!

He had heard the name of Sayyid Qāḍī. He was a mystic who lived in Najaf and had students, among other things.

He got the idea of going to Najaf in order to see Sayyid. He could solve some of his issues by partaking in intense spiritual self-exercise for long periods. He began to work in a morgue to make things even more challenging for himself. As a result, he gained the ability to perform astonishing acts. However, he felt that something needed to be fixed, that his path had somehow been incorrect.

He eventually made Sayyid's acquaintance. "Do you have a wife?" the Sayyid asked him. "No,"he replied, "but I have a mother and sister."

"How do you take care and provide for them?" inquired the Sayyid. "Whatever I require immediately presents itself to me. Look, watch this...." He pointed towards the river with his hand, and immediately a fish jumped out of the water and landed in front of them.

Sayyid Qāḍī smiled. He now understood his problem, "This is not how it works. A Muslim must work and have an occupation. Another fish, please!"

No matter how much he tried, there was no sign of another fish on this occasion. At that moment, he realized that God ﷻ would provide him sustenance, but he had to perform his duties and responsibilities. He then understood that to be in the presence of Sayyid Qāḍī, he had to work and worship and not merely partake in pseudo-spiritual self-exercise.

Story 18: The Visit[7]

For ten years, he was affected by gout. It was so bad that he always had to use a walking stick. "Mr. Limpy" is what he came to be known by the people.

One day, he decided to go to Mashhad and perform the ziyāra of Imām 'Alī al-Riḍā ؑ. On arriving in Mashhad, he suddenly felt no pain in his foot. He began taking steps without the stick.

[7] This story is related to the Sayyid always mentioning to those who were going to Mashhad for the first time that Imām 'Alī al-Riḍā ؑ would grant one of their first three requests, sometimes granting all three. He was then asked about his first three requests, and the above story deals with his first request, i.e., the healing of his foot. (Translator's Note)

Story 19: Without the Night Prayer?

He would always become astonished whenever he heard that a person was going after spirituality but not regularly performing the Night Prayer.

He once wrote to one of his students: "There is no way that a believer and wayfarer can ignore and be heedless of the Night Prayer. It is unfathomable for a person to seek perfection while not being able to wake up for the Night Prayer. We have not heard of any person being able to reach the heights of spirituality except through this Night Prayer."

Story 20: Find an Excuse for your Heart

He would practice and advise the following to his students, "When you wake for the Night Prayer, eat something simple, like tea, *dūgh*[8], or a bunch of grapes. Anything that will bring your body out of tiredness and give you energy and drive to worship." He added, "This act will

[8] A type of yogurt drink (Translator's Note)

prevent the carnal soul *(nafs)* from finding excuses."

Story 21: The Cure for Sorrow

Sayyid Qāḍī was blessed with a child whom he was very fond of. Unfortunately, the child passed away as a result of an electric shock.

One of his students decided to visit him and give his condolences. On seeing the student, Sayyid said, "That child was here before you came and left as soon as you arrived."

In response to the condolences of his student, Sayyid said, "All the sorrow and grief of this world is with us until the moment we lift our hands for the *takbīr*[9] of the prayer."

[9] *Takbīr* is the act of lifting the hand towards the ears and saying *Allahu Akbar* that a Muslim performs in order to begin the prayer (Translator's Note) .

Story 22: Patience in Separation! Never!

The Sayyid would say, "I am surprised that Bābā Ṭāhir[10] has said, 'I am okay with health and pain, proximity and separation, just as all other souls are.' How can he say that if people are okay with distance, he is also okay with it? The lover's patience towards all things is so that the distance and separation of the Beloved are shortened. How is it possible for the lover to also be patient towards the separation from his Beloved?

Imām ʿAlī b. Abī Ṭālib ﷺ says in the supplication of Kumayl thus,

فَهَبْنِي يَا إِلَهِي وَسَيِّدِي وَمَوْلايَ وَرَبِّي صَبَرْتُ عَلَى عَذَابِكَ،
فَكَيْفَ أَصْبِرُ عَلَى فِرَاقِكَ
وَهَبْنِي صَبَرْتُ عَلَى حَرِّ نَارِكَ،
فَكَيْفَ أَصْبِرُ عَنِ النَّظَرِ إِلَى كَرَامَتِكَ

[10] Bābā Ṭāhir was an 11th-century Sufi poet who lived and died in Hamadan, I. R. Iran. (Translator's Note)

Then suppose, My God, my Master, my Protector and my Lord that I am able to endure Your chastisement, but how can I endure separation from You?

And suppose I can endure the heat of Your fire, but how can I endure not gazing upon Your generosity?"

Story 23: Whether it is this World or the Hereafter!

One day, standing outside the school gates, I noticed Sayyid Qāḍī was coming towards me from a distance. On reaching me, he put his hand on my shoulder, looked me in the eyes with a look full of love and kindness, and said, "O my dear boy, if you want this world, perform the Night Prayer; if you want the hereafter, perform the Night Prayer."

He then left.

Story 24: A Night of Laughter

One night I accompanied Sayyid Qāḍī to the Masjid of Sahlah. After praying, we ate some food. He then went to the station attributed to Imām Muḥammad al-Mahdī ﷺ.

It was a cold winter's night, and I watched him the entire time, witnessing his intimate conversations with his Lord and the tears that flowed from his eyes. When morning came, we went to a corner for tea, cheese, and dry flatbread. His state was different.

This is different from the previous night. Then he was telling stories and making funny remarks. He was laughing and making others laugh, so whoever passed by us must have thought we came together to have a good time.

I started to think, "Sayyid Qāḍī and all this joking and laughing...what is happening?"

When we were about to leave, Sayyid Qāḍī turned to me and said, "When you meet people, you must do so with a smile and a happy face. You must open your heart to them and meet them in such a way that it seems the only sorrow you have in your heart is separation from them. You must show kindness to them with every ounce of your existence. However, all of this is good only when done for the pleasure of God. One must be able to feel God's presence and not be heedless of Him during these gatherings and conversations."

Story 25: Look after yourself

Sayyid Qāḍī would often say, "Pay attention to your material affairs as well. Have a spouse and family, and use the blessings God gives you. Travel towards God and find spirituality within this natural and common life."

He always kept his appearance tidy. He would put henna in his hair and hands and even give importance to keeping his shoes clean, while perfume had particular importance to him. He would say, "This physical body is the steed and vehicle of our soul. It must be looked after. The better you care for it, the more it can be used on the path towards God."

Story 26: Pleasure or Necessity

Even though he was never strict concerning the use of worldly blessings and allowed pleasure to be taken from them, he would always advise his students against over-indulgence and over-eating. He constantly said, "Do not eat because it is pleasurable, but rather eat because it is a need and requirement of the body."

Story 27: O He!

My father was very attached to the litany "There is no God, but He.[11]" I would usually hear this recitation coming from his room. Coincidentally, Najaf had pigeons called *'Yā hū'* (O He) during that time. My father liked them very much. He even kept one in the passage between the front gate and the yard.

Story 28: The Breath of Salvation

Qāsim was the most renowned thug in Najaf. He was well-known for his corruption, debauchery, and depravity. Nevertheless, despite all this, Sayyid Qāḍī always treated him incredibly kindly and welcomed him. Because of this treatment, Sayyid Qāḍī was very much respected by him.

---

11 لا اله الا هو

One day, when they bumped into one another, and after all the greetings and niceties, Sayyid Qāḍī said to Qāsim, "You must wake up for the Night Prayer tonight."

"Sayyid, firstly, till midnight, I am at the coffee house. So there is no way that I can interrupt my sleep and wake up for the Night Prayer. Secondly, I do not even pray, and you tell me to wake up for the Night Prayer!"

In response to Qāsim, Sayyid Qāḍī said, "Don't you worry, I will wake you up myself."

Qāsim did not take the Sayyid seriously.

After leaving the coffee house after midnight, he returned home and went to bed. After an hour or so, he wakes up suddenly and goes into the yard. As soon as his eyes hit the water, his entire state changes.

Eventually, this person, known for his sins and vice, became one of Najaf's greatest mystics and ascetics. His reverence reached such a point that people would drink his left-over tea to attain blessings.

Story 29: Open your Eyes! The Path is Clear

One day I asked my teacher, Sayyid Qāḍī, "If we claim that self-knowledge is the shortest path towards reaching God, then why has nothing been specifically mentioned concerning it within the Noble Qur'ān or prophetic traditions?"

He responded, "Is there anything within the divine law that does not have this objective or expedite self-knowledge?"

Story 30: Exegesis of the Noble Qur'ān Through the Noble Qur'ān

Sayyid Qāḍī had a great affinity with the Noble Qur'ān. He was also an exegete of it. He believed that the meaning of the Noble Qur'ān could be attained by benefitting from the Noble Qur'ān itself. He had written an exegesis in this manner from the beginning of the Noble Qur'ān up until the sixth chapter, i.e., Cattle.

The writer of the unmatched contemporary exegesis titled *al-Mīzān*, "Allamah Sayyid

Muḥammad Ḥusayn Ṭabāṭabā'ī ﷺ, confirms that his exegesis was written in the style of his teacher, "This method of Qur'ānic exegesis is from Sayyid Qāḍī. It was he who taught it to us."

Story 31: Respected Sponsor

He went over to thank the builders and architects for their labors in building a portion of the Masjid of Kūfah built because of his efforts. He had barely entered when suddenly the expression on his face changed into one of contempt. He began looking into the distance as if searching for something. His sight fell onto one of the workers. He rushed towards him and took the pickaxe from his hand. Everyone was perplexed. What is happening?

With pickaxe in hand, he rushed towards the sign installed on the wall. Raising the pickaxe, he firmly struck it. As the sign broke and fell, the smile returned to the face of Sayyid Qāḍī.

It became apparent that the builders had written his name on the sign and had installed it on the wall, identifying him as the sponsor of the building work.

Story 32: God Forbid it is my Shoes

It happened to me once before. It made me so embarrassed and uncomfortable. From that time onwards, I made sure to be more attentive.

Whenever I would afterward go to the mourning gatherings held at the house of Sayyid Qāḍī, I would hold onto my shoes and take them inside with me. I feared that if I left them at the door, which is where, on the floor, Sayyid always sat, he would clean them and pair them up as he did for the shoes of the others.

Story 33: Sayyid Qāḍī has caused us to lose this World and the Hereafter!

One of the students of the Sayyid said in jest, "Sayyid Qāḍī has caused us to lose this world and the hereafter. We have not benefited from this world, nor will we from the hereafter."

He was not wrong, for anyone who became acquainted with Sayyid Qāḍī would not show any desire for any of the pleasures of this world or the hereafter; his only concern would be reaching and attaining God ﷻ.

His students often heard him say, "Whoever is only concerned with God, God will ensure that all his other concerns are taken care of."

Story 34: The Test of the Believers

One day I entered the dorms and sat. Sayyid Qāḍī was also sitting there and speaking about the unity of acts[12], that no action can occur independently in this world and without the permission of God ﷻ. Suddenly, in the middle of his discussion, a terrible sound was heard from above the roof, and the room became full of dust and sand.

Confused and in a rush, all the students stormed towards the door of the dorms. Some were pushing others aside so that they could save themselves quicker. After a few moments, it became clear that the roof had not fallen in

---

[12] توحيد افعالی

and that the sound had come from somewhere else.

We all returned to the room and saw that Sayyid Qāḍī had not moved from his place. Coincidentally, the "sound" had come from above his head. As soon as we sat back down, he said, "Perceive, O believers, the unity of acts!"

The sorry state of those students who pushed others aside to save themselves and get to the door quicker was visibly apparent. Indeed, saving one's life is compulsory, but in that situation, we became so heedless of the presence of God ﷻ that we forgot about self-sacrifice and selflessness. We sat there, full of shame and embarrassment.

Story 35: Form

One night, as usual, I woke up for the Night Prayer. However, on this occasion, I felt a strange tiredness. I saw that I could not pray in this state. Suddenly, a beautiful angel appeared in front of me while in this state of uncertainty. On seeing its beauty, all the tiredness that I had, vanished. With ease, I got out of bed, made ablution, and prayed the Night Prayer.

In the morning, I went to see Sayyid Qāḍī and told him what had happened. He remained silent for a while and then said, "Strange! It seems that you are still attached to the form. So when do you intend to reach the meaning and essence?"

The Sayyid would also emphasize not paying attention to these illuminations and unveilings on the path of wayfaring.

He would constantly say, "Give your hearts to God and pay attention to nothing but Him, for everything other than Him will be annihilated. Except Him, nothing else is worthy of being given the heart. When praying or supplicating, ignore the beauty of anything you see or hear. Give all your attention to His Beauty *(Jamāl)* and Absolute Splendor. God forbid, for the sake of Heaven, you become heedless of its Creator."

Story 36 : Say Qāḍī is not coming!

He was known amongst people for his extraordinary feats.

Once he traveled to Najaf, he decided to sit with Sayyid Qāḍī. During their conversation, he told Sayyid, "Previously, I had a state where all plants would tell me their special characteristics. However, it has been some time now that a veil has come between them and me, and they do not speak to me anymore. Please do something so that I can get that state back."

Sayyid responded, "Unfortunately, I can do nothing for you."

He left despondent. Nevertheless, a few days later, he returned and proclaimed, "That which you could not give me, I got from the Imām of the Time. In addition, he told me to tell you that he wants to see you." In a frigid manner, Sayyid Qāḍī responded, "Tell him that Qāḍī is not coming!"

When he left, the Sayyid turned to his students and told them a story of a person whom himself became the initiator of the Shaykhiyah sect and whose student[13] was responsible for creating the deviant Bābism cult.

"The story of this person is like that of Shaykh Aḥmad Aḥsāi'ī[14]. One day, the Shaykh told his students, "Whenever I visit the mausoleum of Imām 'Alī ﷺ and send him my greetings, he replies to me in a loud voice. You all should come with me at least once to hear it for yourselves." His students went with him to the mausoleum. The Shaykh said his greetings and then asked his students, "Did you hear it?" They all replied, "No." He then greeted the Imām for a second time and again asked them if they had heard anything, to which they again replied, "No." It is clear from this that what he had heard were things impregnated into his mind, not really the greetings of the Imām ﷺ."

---

[13] This student is Mirzā 'Alī Muḥammad Shīrāzī (d. 1266 A.H.). He called himself the Bāb or gate to the Imām of the Time ﷺ. His grave is astonishingly located in the city of Haifa, Occupied Palestine, and is a place of visitation. (Translator's Note)

[14] A controversial Shī'a philosopher and scholar of the 12th/13th century. He is buried in the Baqī' Cemetery, Medina. (Translator's Note)

Story 37: Equity

Sayyid Qāḍī had a good and friendly relationship with many of the mystics and gnostics of Najaf; however, he trod very carefully about these relationships.

Concerning one of them, he said, "So and so is like a matchstick. He quickly catches fire and burns out if I mention or explains something beyond his aptitude and ability!"

He even interacted with all his students differently, i.e., he interacted and spoke with them according to their level of ability and aptitude. Some of his students progressed quickly, while others at a slower pace. Some of his students interacted with him for around ten to twelve years, but nothing of true monotheism could be seen from them, while others were only with him for a few years and abruptly left him.

Story 38: Be Happy, O Heart!

On the Day of Ghadīr, he was a completely different person. He would wear fresh clothing and host a festive gathering at home, inviting all his friends and colleagues, serving them sweetmeats, fruits, and much more.

It was tradition for the sermon of Ghadīr to be recited loudly by one of the attendees in this gathering. When it was recited, joy could be seen on the face of Sayyid Qāḍī.

He would also recite poems regarding Ghadīr from memory and even sometimes create one on the spot praising Imām 'Alī ﷷ. On one occasion, he even recited a lengthy poem in Farsi, "Be happy O heart; for happiness has come with Ghadīr, and do not be sad with it only being once a year...."

Story 39: Do not Just Study

In order to continue my studies, I set out toward Najaf from Tabrīz. I had no information regarding the situation in Najaf. I did not know where to go or what to do. Throughout the journey, I considered what subjects to study, the lessons teachers should attend, and what path to choose to earn God's pleasure ﷻ.

When I arrived in Najaf, I immediately turned towards the mausoleum of Imām ʿAlī عليه السلام, "O Imām! I have found my way into your presence to continue my studies, but I do not know which path to take. O my master, I ask you to direct me towards what will benefit me."

On that very first day, I was sitting thinking about my future, and there was a sudden knock on the door. I opened it and saw one of the great scholars of Najaf standing there. I welcomed him in, and he entered and sat down. He had an extraordinarily luminous and attractive face and talked to me with kindness and gentleness. He even recited couplets of poetry for me during our conversation. Then he said, "It is appropriate for anyone wishing to come to Najaf to study that, in addition to their studies, they must also think about self-purification and the perfection of their soul." He said this and left. From that moment, I was pulled toward his mannerisms and moral conduct.

Later on, I came to know that he was Sayyid ʿAlī Qāḍī Ṭabāṭabāʾī.

Story 40: A True Teacher

'Allāmah Ṭabāṭabā'ī would say, "When I first started reading the book *Asfār*[15] of Mullā Ṣadrā,[16] I would spend much time thinking about the philosophical discussions contained within it and analyze and dissect them thoroughly. Slowly but surely, an arrogance took shape within me where I thought that even if Mullā Ṣadrā himself had to reappear, he would not be able to explain and dissect this book the way I have. Then I got the opportunity to attend the classes of Sayyid Qāḍī, and it was when he began explaining the discussion on "existence" that I realized I had not understood a single word of the text."

---

15 An advanced and very sophisticated philosophical text, generally printed in 9 volumes. It is usually the last philosophical textbook that is studied within the seminary. (Translator's Note)

16 Ṣadr al-Dīn Muḥammad b. Ibrahīm Shīrāẓī (aka Mullā Ṣadrā) ﷺ was an 11th-century AH Shī'a philosopher and mystic. His work has greatly influenced and enriched the Islamic intellectual tradition. The book mentioned above, Asfār, can be considered his magnum opus. (Translator's Note)

Story 41: No Benefit Available

With all the travel difficulties of that time, he packed his bags and traveled to Najaf, hoping to benefit from the presence of Sayyid Qāḍī. On arriving in Najaf, before visiting the shrine of Imām 'Alī ☙, he went to the home of the Sayyid. When Sayyid Qāḍī became aware that this individual had abandoned this etiquette[17], he completely distanced himself from him, saying, 'There is no benefit in me for you.'

No matter how much he insisted, Sayyid Qāḍī would not budge from his stance.

Story 42: Have you Verified it?

I had heard certain things concerning Sayyid Qāḍī but was unsure if they were true. Coincidentally, I bumped into him outside the masjid one day. I greeted him, and we had a warm conversation. He began speaking about the secrets of creation, the signs of God ☙, and the elevated station of true monotheism. Again I started to think, "Are there realities that we are

---

[17] That is, first performing the ziyāra of Imām 'Alī ☙.

heedless of? Shame on us! However, how do we know his statement is true?" I was in this chain of thought that suddenly, I saw a huge snake hurtling towards us. I froze in fear. At once, I saw Sayyid Qāḍī point to it and say, "By the permission of God, perish!" The snake halted and became stiff, and so did I. Was this real? Or was I dreaming?

We entered the masjid and did our prayers. While praying, it again occurred to me, '"Was it real what that man did, or was it just an illusion? Did that snake die? Alternatively, is it alive and just fled?"

I exited the masjid and saw that that snake was as stiff as a dried piece of wood lying on the floor. I kicked it, but it did not move. I then went back into the masjid to continue my prayers and acts of worship. When everything was done, I saw Sayyid Qāḍī again. He had a smile on his face and said to me, "My dear, have you verified it?"

Story 43: From the Milk of a Dog to that of a Sheep

I was not someone who looked favorably toward mysticism and mystics. I had heard that Sayyid Qāḍī held lessons on mysticism in Najaf. So, I decided to sit in one of these sessions, and whenever he made mention of a mystical issue, I would stand up and object to it.

One day I went to the masjid where the Sayyid would teach and sat behind a pillar so that he would not notice me. The Sayyid entered and began his lesson, "In the Name of God the All-beneficent, the All-merciful." He then remained silent for a while. Again, he repeated, "In the Name of God, the All-beneficent, the All-merciful." Again he remained silent for a while. He repeated this for a third time. "In the Name of God, the Beneficent, the Merciful. I am surprised by a person who is thirsty, wandering around an arid desert. A bowl is given to him so that he can get milk from a herd of sheep, but instead, he goes towards a pack of dogs and wants to take milk from them!"

When I heard these words, my entire existence began to tremble suddenly. I realized what was going on. I thought to myself, "Why did I come to object? Sitting and listening to what is being said would be better. It may be correct."

I had changed my original intention and felt at ease in that instance. Sayyid Qāḍī then said, "Good, now it has been corrected."

When the lesson finished, I approached Sayyid, kissed his hand, and apologized. He welcomed me warmly, and like this, the door for my interaction with him was opened.

Story 44: Prepared for the Meeting

He wrote a letter to his teacher, complaining about his low spiritual state. His teacher, in response, wrote the cure to his ailment, "My dear brother! All of these issues, such as uncertainty and agitation, are a result of heedlessness[18]. The lowest level of which concerns the ordinances of God. The cause of all heedlessness is being heedless of death and

18 غفلة

imagining you will remain in this world forever. So, to be free from all uncertainty, doubt, and fear, continuously think about your death and prepare for your meeting with God. This is the key to success in this world and the hereafter."

Story 45: Only a Few Handfuls of Water

Only a few people had a bath in their homes during those days. Most would use public bathhouses. In Najaf, there were two bathhouses, the bathhouse of Qayṣariyah and the one of ʿAlī Aghā.

If the Sayyid required a complete ablution[19] at a time when the bathhouses were closed, he would not wait for them to open. He would see this state as being very heavy. He regularly said, "A believer must as quickly as possible exit the heavy state of requiring a full ablution."

In these instances, he would spread a towel in the corner of his room, stand upon it, and according to the prophetic tradition, make the

19 غُسَل

complete ablution with only a few handfuls of water.

Story 46: Pond of the Soul

In the past, sanitation was different from what it is today. In some areas, the water that flowed in the gutters for people to use was often dirty. This water was placed in water stores or ponds until all the dirt and muck settled at the bottom. It was only then that this water was used for washing.

Sayyid Qāḍī would often say to his students, "The soul of a person is similar to that pond. The dirt and muck will settle at the bottom if it is tranquil. But what is the manner of acquiring this tranquility? Silence. When we are talkative and throw ourselves into futile turbulence, what we do in reality shakes our souls. However, if a person observes silence, that pollution that has settled at the bottom will eventually solidify and remain stagnant. In this way, a person can bring his soul under his control...."

Story 47: It brings about Great Illumination!

A person came to see Sayyid and described his state to him. During the conversation, the person said, "Every day, I read five parts of the Noble Qur'ān."

Sayyid Qāḍī responded with amazement, "Five parts! That will bring about great illumination!" He repeated this statement twice.

Amongst the written recommendations of Sayyid Qāḍī, the following words exist, "The daily recitation of the Noble Qur'ān should not be less than one part. I sincerely advise you regarding the recitation of the Noble Qur'ān during the night with a beautiful and sorrowful voice; for such a recitation is the intoxicant of the believer."

Story 48: The Noble Qur'ān under the Blanket

I once asked Sayyid Qāḍī, "Some have claimed that there are individuals who, when they recite the Noble Qur'ān, witness astonishing things and that the horizons of the cosmos appear in front of them. So why is it that we see nothing when we recite it?"

The Sayyid raised his head and said, "Indeed, that person you are describing recites the Noble Qur'ān with its proper etiquettes. They stand facing the *Qiblah*, lift the Noble Qur'ān with both hands, and with their entire existence, pay attention to what they are reciting and in front of whom they are standing. But what do we do? We go under our blankets, pull it up to our chins and then look at the Noble Qur'ān."

At that moment, I recalled how I would recite the Noble Qur'ān; it was just as the Sayyid had described, under the blanket, pulled up to my chin!

Story 49: Time to Sleep

Sayyid Qāḍī slept for four hours, three hours at night, and one hour during the day.

He would say, "The sleep of the people has three stages. The initial stage of sleep begins with them lying down and continues until they achieve a deep sleep. The next stage is this stage of deep sleep, whose appropriate length differs from person to person, depending on age and temperament. This is the primary stage of sleep that the body requires. The third stage is from this deep sleep until the person gets out of bed. If a person is able, through practice and training, to become needless of the first and third stages, all that remains is the second stage, and this stage does not require more than four or five hours."

Story 50: The Prescription

Sayyid Qāḍī would order his students and anyone wishing to travel to God ﷻ to keep a copy of the tradition known as *ʿUnwān al-Baṣrī*[20] in their pockets and read it at least once or twice every week.

The tradition of *ʿUnwān al-Baṣrī* is a complete elixir of instructions concerning spiritual

---

[20] A complete English translation and commentary of this tradition have been published under '*True Servitude and the Reality of Knowledge*'. It is an English translation of a Persian commentary written by the contemporary scholar Āyatullāh Muḥammad Bāqir Taḥrīrī. (Translator's Note)

wayfaring and teachings on how to live one's life in an Islamic and spiritual manner in the blessed words of Imām Jaʿfar al-Ṣādiq ﷺ.

This tradition deals with matters such as social interactions, silence and solitude, food, acquisition of knowledge, and being patient in difficulties, as well as the subtleties of obedience, submission, pleasure, and arriving at the station of true monotheism. All of these matters have been eloquently explained in this tradition.

Sayyid Qāḍī would only accept a person as a student if they were committed to this tradition.

Story 51: With these mannerisms?

He visited Sayyid Qāḍī and requested the Sayyid to acquire permission for him to enter into the presence of the Imām of the Time ﷺ. With a firm look, Sayyid raised his head and said, "How do you expect to reach this level when your behavior is so harsh and bad at home with your family?"

Story 52: Punishment

I said to Sayyid, "There was amongst my students one who did not study properly, so I punished him. I had taken permission from his guardian regarding his discipline. However, he is not here anymore, so I cannot seek his pardon."

"You must find him and seek his pardon; there is no other way."

"I do not know where he stays, nor do I have his address."

The Sayyid said, "To the extent possible, you must try to find him. The doors of spirituality, proximity, and knowledge will remain closed until you remove the responsibility that is upon your shoulders. All these levels are related to God, and He has placed His pleasure and satisfaction in the pleasure and satisfaction of the people."

Story 53: Disrespect

On one of his travels from Najaf to Karbala, Sayyid Qāḍī stayed at our home. When he wished to leave, I escorted him to the door to bid him farewell.

At that time, one of the children also ran out of the house following me, and no matter how hard I tried, the child would not leave me and return.

I then said to Sayyid, "Just let me put this son of a gun back[21] inside and I will return."

Suddenly, Sayyid stopped and asked me, "What did you say?" His face became red, and his hands began to tremble. I have never seen him get this angry before. Very agitatedly, he exclaimed, "This is my child. The word that you used indicates my baseness! I do not want to hear you say such a phrase again! You and your children are all Sayyids and children of the Messenger of

---

[21] The Persian word used is پدرسوخته, lit. of a burnt father, which is a mildly derogatory term, sometimes used in jest. (Translator's Note)

God. Showing disrespect to a Sayyid child is tantamount to disrespecting the Messenger!"

Story 54: Respect

He would always call his children with the prefix of respect, Aghā.

Aghā Sayyid Mahdī

Aghā Sayyid Muḥammad Ḥasan

Aghā Sayyid Taqī

He would always say, "They are the children of the Messenger of God; the time gap between them and he is greater. Even though they are mine, showing them respect and admiration is necessary."

He would even pick up the little kids who would enter his home as a sign of respect for them. He would say, "They are Sayyids, and showing respect to the children of Lady Zahrāʾ is compulsory."

Story 55: Crown

Whenever he wanted to put his turban (*'amāmah*) on his head, he would pick it up with both hands, kiss it and then put it on. Similarly, when he wanted to take it off, he would use both hands, kiss it, and put it neatly to one side.

He would say, "Observing the sanctity of the turban is compulsory. It is the crown of the Messenger of God and the Angels."

Story 56: Play Argument

He was very soft and caring. Not one to be harsh or shout.

However, at times, because of the mischief of his children, he would slightly tell them off. He would show that he was angry, not that he was. One time, after one of those telling-offs, one of his children saw him go into a quiet space and whisper, "My Lord if I shouted, know that it was not real."

Story 57: No Permission

No one could escape his anger. The teacher of the *maktab*[22] was not someone who messed around. He would adequately punish those students who misbehaved.

It was the class of this teacher that we attended. One day, I went home with a swollen face. When my father saw it, he was taken aback.

The next day he went to the maktab, wanting to speak to the teacher. The teacher began to explain, "At times, it is necessary. Without punishment, the children will become defiant. They will not listen to the teacher." My father remained silent.

When the teacher finished speaking, my father said very calmly, "Even if what you say is true, I still do not give you permission to raise your stick at my son."

---

[22] Traditional elementary schooling system of the Islamic World. (Translator's Note)

The teacher went silent. My father understood from his silence that he had not changed his view.

When we returned home, my father said, "You no longer have to go to the maktab. I will teach you myself at home."

Story 58: Wifely Mannerisms

When he got me married, he said, "If you want tranquility in this world and felicity in the hereafter, then when you enter your spouse's home, do not continuously say that you want this and you do not want that.'

This is how we genuinely were. If we had it, we had it; if we did not, we were content and carried on.

Story 59: Mathnawī

He had a special reverence for Rūmī[23]. He read the entire Mathnawī.[24] a reported eight times, and he would understand something new about it each time. He also believed that Rūmī was a pure Shīʿa of Imām ʿAlī ؏; for it was impossible for a person to reach perfection and not witness the reality of divine authority (*wilāyah*).

He would say, "Attaining true monotheism and union can only be achieved via the door of divine authority. They have one reality. Therefore, the well-known mystics were either Shīʿa esoterically or never achieved perfection and union."

---

[23]Jalāl al-Dīn Muḥammad Rūmī Balkhī ؏, aka Mawlānā or Mawlawī, was one of the greatest and most influential mystical poets within the Islamic tradition. He lived during the 7th century AH and is buried in Turkey. (Translator's Note)

[24] This is the famous poetic work of Rūmī. It is written in Persian. (Translator's Note)

Story 60: Good Deeds

"Sayyid! Recently they have brought material and started putting it on the roads such that if water is poured over it, it does not go into the ground." What this person meant was asphalt that was newly brought to Najaf. He wanted to see Sayyid Qāḍī's reaction to the roads being asphalted. He may have thought that this teacher of mysticism would be indifferent to this new advancement.

Sayyid Qāḍī very clearly replied, "This for the wayfarer towards God is a good thing. It will make performing good deeds easier."

Story 61: I am Here!

Once, a photographer came to take pictures of Sayyid Qāḍī. He then developed and brought them to him. Then, the students of Sayyid Qāḍī would not leave him alone.

After a while, the photographer got up to leave, but he was followed out by the Sayyid students, who hoped to get a picture for themselves.

Sayyid Qāḍī, who was sitting in the corner of the room, smiled and said to them, "I am sitting here in the flesh! However, you are chasing after a picture of me!"

Story 62: Bright

Sayyid Qāḍī was a model of cleanliness and neatness.

His turban and clothes were always clean. No stain or dirt was seen on his clothes for fifty years since he was in Najaf. Whether it was summer or winter, his clothes would always be bright.

Story 63: Cleaner

During those days in Najaf, the groundwater was both salty and dirty. Clean drinking water had to be brought from Kūfah.

One day I was sitting next to the school's pond, wanting to perform ablution, when I saw Sayyid Qāḍī. He had a water container in his hand and wanted to do ablution with it. I thought, "Why does he not take ablution with normal water like the rest of us?"

He asked me, "Do you have drinking water in your dormitory?" "Yes, I do," I replied.

He asked, "So why don't you perform ablution with that water?" I saw this as an opportunity, so I said, "The water in the pond is clean, and everyone performs ablution with it." He smiled, "True, but that water is cleaner."

Story 64: Prevention

Malaria was endemic to Najaf, So the government officials decided to destroy the ponds that people would have in their homes in order for them to get used to using water from the reservoir. Some "traditionalists" and fanatics did not buy into this proposal. They argued, "The water in the pond is clean and usable. So why do we have to use another source of water?"

When Sayyid Qāḍī became aware of the issue, he immediately picked up a pickaxe, destroyed the pond in his house, and said, "This is the request of the government, and it is a rational request."

He did this at a time when the government of Iraq did not allow themselves to enter the homes of the scholars or dignitaries and would only inspect the homes of the common folk.

Story 65: Impenetrable Armor

I asked, '"If one, be it in his worldly or spiritual affairs, reaches a dead end and helpless situation, what litany should he recite in order for it to be resolved?"

"First, send salutations upon the Noble Prophet and his Family five times[25], then recite the verse of the Throne[26] five times. Then recite the following litany within your heart, without verbally reciting it, to such an extent that the issue or issues are resolved."

[25] اللَّهُمَّ صَلِّ عَلَى مُحَمَّدٍ وَ آلِ مُحَمَّدٍ

[26] Sūrat al-Baqarah, Verse 255.

﴿اللَّهُ لا إِلَٰهَ إِلّا هُوَ الحَيُّ القَيّومُ ۚ لا تَأخُذُهُ سِنَةٌ وَلا نَومٌ ۚ لَهُ ما
فِي السَّماواتِ وَما فِي الأَرضِ ۗ مَن ذَا الَّذي يَشفَعُ عِندَهُ إِلّا بِإِذنِهِ
ۚ يَعلَمُ ما بَينَ أَيديهِم وَما خَلفَهُم ۖ وَلا يُحيطونَ بِشَيءٍ مِن عِلمِهِ
إِلّا بِما شاءَ ۚ وَسِعَ كُرسِيُّهُ السَّماواتِ وَالأَرضَ ۖ وَلا يَئودُهُ حِفظُهُما
ۚ وَهُوَ العَلِيُّ العَظيمُ﴾

﴿*allāhu lā ʾilāha ʾillā huwa l-ḥayyu l-qayyūmu lā taʾkhudhuhū sinatun wa-lā nawmun lahū mā fī s-samāwāti wa-mā fī l-ʾarḍi man dhā lladhī yashfaʿu ʿindahū ʾillā bi-ʾidhnihī yaʿlamu mā bayna ʾaydīhim wa-mā khalfahum wa-lā yuḥīṭūna bi-shayʾin min ʿilmihī ʾillā bi-mā shāʾa wasiʿa kursiyyuhu s-samāwāti wa-l-ʾarḍa wa-lā yaʾūduhū ḥifẓuhumā wa-huwa l-ʿaliyyu l-ʿaẓīmu*﴾

﴿*God—there is no god except Him— is the Living One, the Sustainer. Neither drowsiness befalls Him nor sleep. To Him belongs whatever is in the heavens and whatever is on the earth. Who is it that may intercede with Him except with His permission? He knows that which is before them and that which is behind them, and they do not comprehend anything of His knowledge except what He wishes.*

His seat embraces the heavens and the earth, and He is not wearied by their preservation, and He is the Exalted, the Supreme﴿

اللَّهُمَّ اجْعَلْنِي فِي دِرْعِكَ الْحَصِينَةِ الَّتِي تَجْعَلُ فِيهَا مَنْ تَشَاءُ

'O God! Place me within Your impenetrable armor, in which You place whomever You desire.'

Story 66: Whether Given or Whether Taken

ʿAllāmah Ṭabāṭabāʾī ﵀ once said, "During my studies in Najaf, there came a time when communication with Iran became very difficult. As a result, I was no longer allowed to receive the money I had used to cover my living expenses.

My living conditions slowly started to become very difficult. I was under severe pressure and was very aggrieved.

One day I thought to myself, why do I not go to my teacher, Sayyid Qāḍī, and explain my situation? Maybe he can assist me in coming out of this back-breaking condition.

So I went and opened my heart to him. There was a lot I had to get off my chest when I had laid out all my problems before him. He raised his head and smiled. He advised me and said things that completely flipped my state. A while later, when I wanted to leave, I felt such a lightness as if I had no problem in my life. When I reached home, I sat down and composed his advice as a poem."

Anxiety took over me last night.

The thorn of sorrow pierced my heart

In front of my wise teacher, I sat

All my sorrow and grief to him did I present

It was like he had an action plan at hand

Possessing the vibrancy of youth and wisdom of old

My wise and luminous guide

Removed from my heart the sorrowful tide

Be free in your life, said he

This world will pass, have glee

To yourself, attribute existence, not

To your heart glitz and glamor, give not

For what you do not possess, why worry?

From grief and sorrow, why make your heart flurry?

In His hand is what is given and taken

In His ownership is what is established and destroyed

Be the state of sorrow effective or ignored

The pen of destiny straight will remain

Whatever God wills will come to pass

Not that which your heart desires

Story 67: Persevere

Whenever one of his students became despondent or tired, the Sayyid would reenergize them with these words, "For forty years I remained patient, waiting for the door of reality to open for me, and eventually it did. If you are truly seeking the Truth, continue your search. If you have not reached it yet, you eventually will. Do not allow doubt into your heart. Do not be satisfied and content for just a little when the door opens for you. Seek further and try to achieve more. A person may scratch the surface, but a spring of pure water suddenly comes gushing out."

Story 68: Sayyid Rūḥullāh!

On that day, around ten or fifteen students were in the ethical class of Sayyid Qāḍī. We noticed that a young Sayyid had entered the room and went to sit quietly in one of the corners. Usually, Sayyid would stand in respect for a guest and request them to sit at the front, but on this occasion, the environment was burdensome and cold.

The young Sayyid, with absolute respect, sat with his knees on the floor. Sayyid Qāḍī remained silent. The room was silent for nearly fifteen minutes, with both sayyids having their heads down.

All of a sudden, Sayyid Qāḍī turned to me and said, "Shaykh ʿAbbās, please bring me that book." I forgot to ask which book, but intrinsically my hand went towards a book, which I then brought to the Sayyid. "Open it," he said.

"To which page?" I asked. "Any page."

So I opened the book to a page with the word "Anecdote" written at the top. I began to read that anecdote out aloud. It was a very fascinating one.

"There was once a kingdom that a sultan ruled. This sultan and his family were enveloped by corruption, vice, and irreligiosity. A man of God stood up against this sultan. No matter how much he advised the sultan, there was no use, so he was forced to take harsher measures against him. The sultan ordered that the godly man be arrested and put into prison. He was then exiled to one of the neighboring kingdoms. After some time, that godly man was exiled to a kingdom that housed the shrines of the Imāms ﷷ. A time will come when that sultan will flee, thus allowing the godly man to return to his land and take the reins of government in his hands....'

Here, Sayyid Qāḍī said, "That will do. Close the book and return it to its place." Then, Sayyid began to speak. He talked about the corruption and tribulations that would come in the future. The young Sayyid got up and left when the session ended, but we were still stunned by what had just happened. Why was the gathering held in that manner?

It was only years later, when news started coming in about the occurrences that were happening in Iran that this incident became clearer for those who were present, such as Shaykh 'Abbās Qūchānī, who was Sayyid Qāḍī's religious representative after his passing.

When Sayyid Khumaynī ﵀ was exiled to Najaf, Shaykh 'Abbās went to meet him. On seeing him for the first time, he recognized him as being that young Sayyid from that day.

Shaykh 'Abbās was also one of the first people who traveled to Iran after the victory of the Islamic Revolution and gave his oath of allegiance to Sayyid Khumaynī قدس سره.

The unusual behavior of Sayyid Qāḍī on that day may have been a means to test the spiritual resolve of Sayyid Khumaynī قدس سره. It is said that when Sayyid Khumaynī قدس سره was asked outside about that session, "How did you find Sayyid Qāḍī?" He replied, "He is a person of great stature, greater than I thought he would be!"

Even afterward, he would say about him, "Sayyid Qāḍī was a mountain of grandeur and a pillar of pure monotheism."

Story 69: Dervish

Some scholars of Najaf gathered stones and threw them at the door of Sayyid Qāḍī. They would tell students that if they joined his classes, they would never attain *ijtihād.* They would speak ill about him in the presence of the jurist consultants of the time. The students who interacted with him would have their monthly student stipend cut by them. They even exiled some of his students from Najaf. They would break the lamps of the masjid he would teach in, stop him from praying, and throw stones at the places he used to teach.

They would proclaim, "Qāḍī is a dervish and misguides the students." However, they knew that the path of Sayyid Qāḍī was nowhere close to the dervishes of that time.

Some of the dervishes of that time, with the excuse of having attained the station of true monotheism or divine authority, would not adhere to the religious and jurisprudential laws as they ought to. Sayyid Qāḍī was a jurist in his own right and firmly believed that the only way to attain the station of true monotheism and mystical realities was via religious law and its observance. There was not even a recommended act that he would not perform.

Those who opposed him would use this as a sign of his hypocrisy, "This asceticism and performance of the recommended acts of worship that is seen from Qāḍī are not done out of sincerity. He is just a Sufi, and Sufis do not see any value or benefit in these acts."

In the face of all these accusations and ill-treatment, Sayyid Qāḍī would advocate patience and forbearance from his students. However, he also took steps to try and correct the misunderstandings.

Sometimes he would say, "Our path is the same as that of the scholars and jurists...plain and simple...." Once someone asked him about the chain of his teachers, he replied, "We are nothing like the dervishes...do not create a chain for me."

In addition, the clothes he wore, the food he ate, and the social interactions he had had no similarity with the ways of the dervishes; however, this accusation of being a dervish was the best weapon in the arsenal of his opponents.

Story 70: Worry

Whenever he would go to the mausoleum of Imām ʿAlī ﷷ, he would always recite the ziyāra. On this one occasion, we noticed that when we visited the mausoleum, he left without reciting it. So I asked him, "Why have you left so quickly today?"

"I saw someone in the mausoleum who I know has a hatred for me in his heart. I feared this hatred would again erupt in his heart if he saw me and nullified his good deeds."

Story 71: Flagbearer

He came in panting as if he had run the whole way. In his mind, he thought he was bringing some important news. "They spoke ill of you in the presence of Sayyid Abū Ḥasan Iṣfahānī [27]. He also then ordered that whoever studies anything other than jurisprudence and its principles will have their monthly stipend cut, including you and your students."

Sayyid Abū Ḥasan Iṣfahānī was the head of the Najaf seminary and the jurist consultant of the Shīʻa world at the time.

Sayyid Qāḍī looked at his student with a look full of serenity and said, "Respecting and obeying the order of Sayyid Abū Ḥasan Iṣfahānī

---

[27] Āyatullāh Sayyid Abū Ḥasan Iṣfahānī was a great scholar and jurist of the 13th/14th century AH. He passed away in 1365 AH and is buried within the mausoleum of Imām ʻAlī. (Translator's Note)

ؒ is compulsory on all. He is the flagbearer of Islam, and it is the responsibility of all to assist him in any way possible."

Story 72: I am Not That Person

On arriving in Najaf from Iran, they went to the house of Sayyid Qāḍī as a sign of respect. When they met him, they said, "Sayyid, we take you as our jurist consultant." Tears began to form in the eyes of Sayyid Qāḍī, and his whole demeanor changed. He then lifted his hands and said, "O Lord! You know that I am not that person they say I am!" He then turned to them and said, "Go and take Sayyid Abū Ḥasan Iṣfahānī ؒ as your jurist consultant."

Story 73: Mum's the Word

One of the well-known scholars of Mashhad had an extraordinary hatred for my father. Speaking ill of my father was his favorite topic, from the pulpit to the Blessed Month of Ramaḍān. He did not know who I was, and I did not say anything either; I only had a pen and paper to take notes.

One day it was said to him, "Do you know that his son is sitting in your lectures?" He then approached me, apologized, and even invited me to breakfast at his home.

I returned to Najaf and showed my notes to my father. On seeing them, he said, "Have you gone crazy? So and so never speaks like this. Go and throw these papers away!"

This incident passed. Thirty years later, a book of this same scholar came to my attention, and it put what he was saying in Mashhad to shame!

Āyatullāh Bahjat ؒ once said, "So and so (this same scholar from Mashhad) would curse a person who I knew would cry so much before going to sleep out of love and fear of God that his pillow would become wet. However, I have heard that he sought forgiveness before the end of his life."

Story 74: I am not Happy!

'"Shaykh Ibrāhīm! It has come to my attention that you mentioned my name from the pulpit at the house of so and so, and so you mentioned my name?"

Before then, I had never seen the face of Sayyid so agitated and aggrieved. "Yes, Sayyid, I did...."

Then the Sayyid continued, "If you believe in the allowed and the forbidden, I am not happy that my name is mentioned, not on the pulpit, not off it...it is forbidden for any of these brothers who attend my classes to exaggerate about me; I am not okay with it."

Story 75: Shoe Sole!

Once, someone asked him, "Are you a Perfect Man (*insān al-kāmil*)?" He answered, "I am not worthy of even being the sole of the shoe of the Perfect Man."

He always saw himself as being nothing.

Story 76: Go and Listen!

I was walking behind the Sayyid when suddenly, I saw a shaykh approaching us from afar. He stopped before the Sayyid and said, "How do we know what you are saying is correct? I want to hear these things from the mouth of Imām Muḥammad al-Mahdī عجل الله تعالى فرجه الشريف myself." "Fine, let us go and hear them," was the answer he heard. He stood there, stunned. He never expected such a response.

We set off; I was walking behind them when, all of a sudden, I noticed that our surroundings had changed. We were now walking in a desert. After a while, a rising started to become apparent on the horizon. People were also frequenting it.

The shaykh quickly regretted his decision. "Take me back! I do not want to go anymore!"

"But it was you who insisted on going and seeing for yourself," responded the Sayyid. He replied panicky, "No! Please take me back!"

So we turned back from that place. It was not long before we found ourselves back in familiar surroundings.

Story 77: Sacred Soil

"There is no God, but God; there is no God, but God; there is no God, but God...."

He was busy with this litany when suddenly the string of his rosary, with beads made from the soil of Karbala, snapped. The beads scattered all over the floor. His weak eyesight made it impossible for him to collect them. Regardless, he stayed up the entire night trying to find them, in reverence of the soil of Imām al-Ḥusayn 𓆣, lest he might stretch his legs towards it.

Story 78: Sayyid Ḥasan

He sought permission from the Sayyid and entered. When Sayyid saw who it was, his eyes lit up. He loved this individual very much. He was one of the strong students of Sayyid Qāḍī, and very few could teach philosophy and mysticism as he could. He was Sayyid Ḥasan from the capital city of 'Umān, Masqaṭ.

When he would sit in the courtyard of Imām 'Alī 𓆣 and speak about true monotheism, a fantastic feeling would enter the hearts of the listeners. His words would enliven the stale souls but also awakens jealousy in others.

It reached a point when some of these individuals spoke badly about him to Sayyid Abū Ḥasan Iṣfahānī ؒ. He now came to his teacher for advice on what to do. "Sayyid Abū Ḥasan has forbidden me from teaching philosophy and mysticism. He has ordered me to return to Masqaṭ and propagate there. However, leaving Najaf and you is not easy for me. Grant me permission to continue my lessons and ignore the command of Sayyid Iṣfahānī ؒ. Should I stand firm on the path of true monotheism?"

Sayyid Qāḍī smiled at him and said, "As per the command of Sayyid Abū Ḥasan, leave Najaf and go to Masqaṭ. God is with you; no matter where you are, He will guide you and take you to the highest levels of monotheism and knowledge."

When the time came for his departure, Sayyid Qāḍī came to bid him farewell. When he saw that Sayyid Ḥasan was upset, he said,

'"Wherever the friend of God is, there are the people of divine authority, So it makes no difference where you are."

Sayyid Ḥasan, first in Masqaṭ, then in India, was a source of excellent good and blessings. He also trained many students.

Many years later, when the news of the passing of Sayyid Ḥasan was telegraphed to Najaf, none of the students of Sayyid Qāḍī dared to inform him. Eventually, it was decided that Sayyid Hāshim Ḥaddād ؏ should inform him. However, when the news was given to Sayyid Qāḍī, he said, "I already knew."

Story 79: Last Will

He believed that praying on time aided in the development of man, such that if a person were to observe it continuously, they would reach perfection. "If a person were to pray his compulsory prayers on time regularly and yet does not reach a lofty station, he can send curses upon me!"

He also firmly believed that even a prayer without the presence of a heart prayed on time would correct the affairs of the one performing it.

He wrote his last will on several occasions. In his final one, that is dated 12th Safar 1365 AH[28] i.e., about one year before his passing, he wrote,

"...Another piece of advice, specifically regarding the prayer. Do not take the prayer lightly. Pray it on time, with humbleness and presence of the heart. If you can protect your prayer, everything else will be protected. Regularly perform the tasbīḥ of Sayyidah Fāṭimah al-Zahrā' 🌸 and Āyatul Kursī after your prayers.

Do not neglect the ziyāra of Imām al-Ḥusayn 🌸 for the recommended acts. The holding of the weekly mourning gathering, even if it is just 2-3 people, is a means for opening the doors of one's affairs. If one were to spend their entire life serving this great personality in the form of mourning or performing the ziyāra, know that you will never be able to give him his due. If the

---

[28] January 16th, 1946

weekly mourning gatherings are not possible, ensure that at least the first ten days of Muḥarram are observed.

It is also necessary for me to advise regarding the following. Obedience to parents, good conduct, always being truthful, the conformity of one's exterior with one's interior, abandonment of deceit and deception, always greeting first, being good to all, be they good or bad, except in instances where God has prohibited it.

I implore you, by God, not to hurt the heart of anyone. Attach hearts towards you as much as possible, for breaking them is not difficult."

Story 80: What if I am not allowed?

During the last days of his life, Sayyid wrote to one of his students, "It has been a few days now that my mind has been occupied with this thought, that if in Paradise I am not allowed to pray, what will I do?"

Story 81: It wants to leave

During his last days, he would sometimes wake up in the middle of the night and recite the Noble Qurʾān or the Mathnawī loudly. Once, when I went to turn the lamp on for him in his room, he said to me, "The room is already full of light; you just cannot perceive it...."

I remember vividly saying to him the day before his passing, "It seems you have a strange state; you sleep, you sit and recite the Noble Qurʾān...."

He replied with a bright face and broad smile, pointing to his chest, "This wants to leave."

Story 82: Ease

He summoned me the night before he passed. His face was glowing outstandingly. "I am in the state of death," he said, lying down, with the soles of his feet facing the *Qiblah*.

He told me not to wake up his wife and other children but to sit beside his head and recite the Noble Qurʾān till morning.

Usually, when someone knows their father is about to leave this world, they will become very emotional and uneasy. However, I accepted this matter comfortably and did not tell anyone else.

I sat and began reciting the Noble Qur'ān. After a short while, he said, "I am starting to feel at ease. This ease has begun from my feet and is making its way upwards. Only my heart is sore." I listened to his words in a very regular manner, as if nothing strange was happening. A few moments later, he told me, "Cover my face." So I did.

He passed away a few moments later, but I found myself calm and relaxed. I continued reciting the Noble Qur'ān until morning.

The morning prayer arrived; the rest of the family came to ask about my father's state. I described to them what had occurred the previous night. It was only then when the house became full of cries and wailing that what had just happened occurred to me. It was as if he made me remain calm and unemotional in that situation, so I could recite the Noble Qur'ān beside him.

Story 83: Responsibility

It was the morning after the passing of Sayyid Qāḍī - 6th Rabīʿ al-Awwal 1366 AH.[29]- and we began thinking about what to do, from where do we start? To whom do we speak? What do we do regarding the Qur'ān reciting gathering for him?

While in this uncertain and worried state, we suddenly saw two or three men approaching us from across the road.

When they arrived at the house, one said, "I went to visit the shrine of Imām al-Ḥusayn ﷺ in the morning, when tiredness came over me, and I took a short nap. I saw someone in my dream telling me to go to Najaf as Sayyid Qāḍī has just passed and to take care of all the funeral arrangements. So I have come to Najaf, and through asking and inquiring, I found you.'

Hājj Yaḥyā ʿIbādī Sajjādī was one of the esteemed personages of Tehran that had come to Iraq during that period to visit the shrines of

---

[29] Circa. February 1947 (Translator's Note)

the Ahl al-Bayt ﷺ. He had no previous acquaintance with Sayyid Qāḍī. He took charge and managed everything. After performing ghusl al-mayyit on Sayyid's body, funeral prayer, and circumambulation of the mausoleum of Imām 'Alī ؑ, he set off towards *Wadī al-Salām.*[30] cemetery. He then went to a location where Sayyid Qāḍī is currently buried, close to the burial place of the Prophets Hūd and Ṣaliḥ ؑ. I asked him, '"How did you know about this location?" "I saw this place in my dream," was his reply.

He remained till the seventh. He also provided the food for that day and left.

Story 84: Both Crying and Cursing

The funeral procession of Sayyid Qāḍī was unique. Some were crying beside the coffin, while others were cursing. These very individuals declared him an apostate when he was alive.

---

[30] It is the biggest cemetery in the world. Located in Najaf, Iraq, close to the shrine of Imām 'Alī ؑ. (Translator's Note)

Story 85: Friend of God

A night before the passing of Sayyid Qāḍī, someone saw in a dream that a coffin with the following phrase, "A friend of God has departed, was being carried away."

Āyatullāh Khū'ī says that he saw with his own eyes that on the night of Sayyid's demise, it was as if the stars in the night sky were falling.

Story 86: I am Good

I remember that when my father passed away, I cried for a long time, nearly four months.

The neighbors even started to get annoyed by it. Until one day, I saw my father in a dream. He was standing in a room and called me, "Fāṭimah!"

"Yes, dear father!"

With his hands over his chest, he asked me, "Why are you crying? I am, all praise be to God, good. Do not be upset...."

It was from this moment that I became calm.

Story 87: A Gift

It was the day of 'Īd[31]. With a few friends, we decided to visit the grave of our teacher, Sayyid Qāḍī. When we reached the grave, one of the brothers addressed Sayyid Qāḍī, saying, "Today is 'Īd, so we want an 'Īd gift from you." Suddenly, while we were all awake, we saw Sayyid Qāḍī come in front of us with his turban and cloak, holding a pitcher of rose water. He then poured that rose water over our hands. In front of our astonished eyes, he said, "I requested from God that he allow me to have control of my body in purgatory."

Story 88: Guidance

My life fell into extreme difficulty, and I could not bear it anymore. I began to think I should end these problems and escape from this life altogether. I wanted to make the form of this issue legitimate.

---

[31] It seems that it was 'Id Nawrūz or the Iranian New Year (Translator's Note)

One night I saw Sayyid Qāḍī in a dream. He told me, "These issues are part of your spiritual wayfaring that God has decreed for you...If you wish to progress, you must live with and bear them."

Story 89: The First Step

We were in Āyatullāh Bahjat قدس سره presence when one of those present asked, "Shaykh, please give us a piece of advice we may benefit from."

Āyatullāh Bahjat قدس سره, whose head was down on hearing this statement, raised it and said, "Have you properly benefitted from that which you have already learned?" He said, "Praise be to God, all of you pray your daily prayers, but have you truly spiritually and mystically benefitted from this act, an act that is the pillar of religion and the source of proximity to God? Do you feel the effects of it in your souls? When we were in the presence of our teacher, Sayyid Qāḍī, this is what he would say to us. We only truly understood the meaning of this point after lengthy spiritual self-excises and deep contemplation. The first step must be taken with honesty and purity. The best starting point is this very prayer.

Regarding the second step, if you do not know what it is, God will, out of His generosity, send someone to teach you."

As he left, he began whispering the following verse of the Noble Qurʾān.

﴿وَالَّذِينَ جاهَدوا فينا لَنَهدِيَنَّهُم سُبُلَنا ۚ وَإِنَّ اللَّهَ لَمَعَ المُحسِنينَ﴾

﴿wa-lladhīna jāhadū fīnā la-nahdiyannahum subulanā wa-ʾinna llāha la-maʿa l-muḥsinīna﴾

﴿As for those who strive in Us, We shall surely guide them in Our ways, and God is indeed with the virtuous﴾[32]

[32] Sūrat al-ʿAnkabūt, Verse 69.

Practical Advice Concerning Observing the Sacred Months[33]

Praise is only for God, the Lord of creation, and may His choicest blessings and salutations. Those of His nearest angels and all of creation, be upon His evident Messenger, the Noble Prophet ﷺ, and also upon his trustworthy viceregent and deputy, Amīr al-Mu'minīn 'Alī b. Abī Tālib ؑ, and upon their purified children ؑ, the rightly guided leaders and guides towards the Real and the Straight path. Blessings and salutations also are upon their pure and rightful inheritor, whose existence is the hope of the Muslim community and the Shī'a. Blessings and salutations are upon them all.

Take heed! The sacred months have descended upon you, so awaken from your slumber! Value and make use of this opportunity to prepare for your journey!

Stay awake during their nights and pass their days fasting. Be thankful that God has, during

[33] What is meant are the three months of Rajab, Sha'bān, and the Blessed Month of Ramaḍān (Translator's Note)

these times, expanded and included all within His mercy.

Only spend a small amount of the night for rest and sleep. Pray the Night Prayer in the manner of *tahajjud,* i.e., pray a few units of prayer, then go to sleep for a bit, then wake again to continue the prayer, and so on. Many lovers will forsake sleep altogether.

Calmly recite the Noble Qur'ān in your best possible voice, as this will change the darkness and crust that has formed on your heart into light. For you, nor anyone else, will have benefited from anything quite like the benefit of the Noble Qur'ān. If anyone says other than what I have said, they are in clear error and have a deviant perception.

Ask God to send abundant blessings and salutations upon the substance and subsidiaries of the Noble Qur'ān.[34] They are the last of the People of God. Be in complete obedience to them and submit to them as if you have no will of your own.

---

34 That is the Noble Prophet, Muḥammad ﷺ, and his Immaculate Family ﵌ (Translator's Note)

Whoever, without their love, sees themselves within the grace of God, or has a speck of love for others other than them in their hearts, is indeed misguided and has denied the divine blessings of their authority. Furthermore, because of this denial, they have lost God's divine blessings.

Hence, love for them is love for God; in this way, one must enter the divine refuge of God's love.

Do not take matters regarding the Noble Qur'ān lightly. Do not recite it as a play or a pastime. Pay attention to its meanings; by doing so, you will be able to reach the highest peaks of honor and dignity.

Incumbent upon you is always to remember God. Let not your busyness with the material world cause you to be lax in the recitation of the Noble Qur'ān and His remembrance, nor let it allow you to make excuses such as how and how much...

These months are God's sanctified forts, so enter them but ensure you venerate them and observe their sanctity; mandate their etiquettes upon yourself.

Know that whoever attaches themselves to the mercy, beauty, and grandeur of God will indeed find themselves on His path. Dear brother! If you were to say, 'God is my Lord,' then stand firm on this statement! Never abandon it!

God says in the Noble Qur'ān,

﴿وَمَن يَعتَصِم بِاللّٰهِ فَقَد هُدِيَ إِلىٰ صِراطٍ مُستَقيمٍ﴾

﴾wa-man yaʿtaṣim bi-llāhi fa-qad hudiya ʾilā ṣirāṭin mustaqīm^in^﴿

﴾And whoever takes recourse in God is certainly guided to a straight path﴿[35]

And He also says,

﴿وَاستَقِم كَما أُمِرتَ﴾

﴾wa-staqim ka-mā ʾumirta﴿

[35] Sūrat Āl ʿImrān, Verse 101.

﴿*and* be steadfast, *just as* you *have been commanded*﴾[36]

And,

﴿إِنَّ الَّذِينَ قالوا رَبُّنَا اللَّهُ ثُمَّ استقاموا تَتَنَزَّلُ عَلَيهِمُ المَلائِكَةُ أَلَّا تَخافوا وَلا تَحزَنوا وَأَبشِروا بِالجَنَّةِ الَّتي كُنتُم توعَدونَ﴾

﴿*'inna lladhīna qālū rabbunā llāhu thumma staqāmū tatanazzalu ʿalayhimu l-malā'ikatu 'allā takhāfū wa-lā taḥzanū wa-'abshirū bi-l-jannati llatī kuntum tūʿadūna*﴾

﴿*Indeed those who say, 'Our Lord is God!' and then remain steadfast, the angels descend upon them, [saying,] 'Do not fear, nor be grieved! Receive the good news of the paradise which you have been promised*﴾[37]

Know, my dear and beloved brothers - may God make you all successful towards his obedience - that we have entered the very sacred territory and, just like we must abstain from performing

---

[36] Sūrat al-Shūrā, Verse 15.

[37] Sūrat Fuṣṣilat, Verse 30.

that which is forbidden in the blessed lands and refrain from performing certain acts that in other lands are allowed, so to must we in these months, for they are counted as the blessed and sacred times of God. So, we must enter them with guardedness and attention and in the same manner as we would enter the sacred and blessed lands. In the blessed land, Man gets close to the House of God (the *Kaʿbah*), whereas in these months, the blessed times, Man reaches the station of nearness to God. How great and magnanimous has God blessed us! He has indeed completed all His favors towards us!

Now that this is the case, the first thing that becomes incumbent and essential upon us is seeking repentance (*tawbah*); repentance contains all the necessary conditions for it to be accepted and the known prayers associated with it.[38].

After repentance, the next most incumbent thing on us is to abstain from performing minor and major sins to the extent of our abilities.

---

[38] That is, the major ablution and prayer of repentance mentioned by the Noble Prophet] on the first Sunday of Dhil al-Qa'dah, the 11th month of the Islamic lunar calendar. This prayer consists of four units, to be prayed in two sets of two each. It is performed as follows: First, make the major ablution, followed by the minor ablution. Then perform two sets of two units of prayer. In each unit, recite the following chapters from the Noble Qur'ān: al-Fātiḥah (The Opening) once, al-Ikhlāṣ (Monotheism) thrice and al-Falaq (Daybreak), and al-Nās (Humans) once each.
After completing the four units, a person should seek repentance seventy times using litanies such as أَسْتَغْفِرُ اللّٰهَ (I seek God's forgiveness). Then the following supplication should be recited once, لاَ حَوْلَ وَلاَ قُوَّةَ إِلاَّ بِاللّٰهِ ٱلْعَلِيِّ ٱلْعَظِيمِ (There is no power, nor might except God's; the All-Exalted, the All-Supreme).
The prayer is then ended with the following supplication, recited once:
يا عَزيزُ يا غَفّارُ إغفِر لِی ذُنُوبِی وَ ذُنُوبَ جَميعِ المؤمِنينَ وَ المُؤمِناتِ فَإنَّهُ لا يَغفِرُ الذُّنُوبَ إلّا أنتَ (O the Impenetrable, the Oft-forgiving, forgive my sins and those of all the believing men and women, for indeed there is no forgiver of sins except you!) (Translator's Note)

Then, dear brothers, perform the advised acts of repentance[39] on the first Thursday night of Rajab, the first Friday, or the first Sunday. It is then to be repeated on the second Sunday of the month.

After making scrutiny (*murāqabah)* incumbent upon yourself, whether it be the minor form, i.e., refraining from all that which God is not pleased with, or the major form, i.e., protecting the heart from that which the Beloved dislikes. In addition, mandate yourself to take account of your actions (*muḥāsibah)*, admonish yourself, where it is necessary, for your actions (*mu'ātibah),* and even punish yourselves for performing a sin with that which is worthy and beneficial *(mu'āqibah)*. In these steps, there is a remembrance for the one who wishes to remember or truly fear God.

After this stage, turn your hearts towards God, cure your spiritual ailments, and through seeking forgiveness and repentance, lessen the load of your big and heavy faults.

---

[39] See note 34 (Translator's Note)

Ensure you refrain from destroying God's sanctuary and breaking the sanctity of His refuge that He has opened for you. In reality, a person who does such is ontological without honor and dignity, even though God, out of His infinite mercy, will protect his apparent dignity and honor. This is the very recompense of this person. There will be no further need for God to do so.

Where can that heart, who has entered it with doubt and ill conviction, find hope of salvation? (That is, one of the definite necessities for a spiritual wayfarer is certainty and conviction of the origin and death (Resurrection), of the reality of the spiritual path and master. If there appears the slightest doubt regarding these things, the wayfarer will automatically stop moving. Hence, the wayfarer cannot find salvation from destruction with the existence of doubt and uncertainty.)[40] Such a person will never be able to set foot on the path of the Godwary, nor will he have the ability to reach

---

[40] This explanation in brackets which appears in the text, is from Sayyid Muḥammad Ḥusayn Tihrānī 颂, one of the students of Sayyid Qāḍī (Translator's Note)

the station of the Virtuous and drink with them from the clear water.

Only God is our helper, and He is the best of helpers.

Now, the practical instructions for these three months:

1. Ensure that you pray your compulsory daily and supererogatory prayers at their most virtuous times. The total unit of these prayers is fifty-one units[41]. If performing all fifty-one is impossible, then at least forty-four units should be read. However, if your occupation with the material world prevents you from doing this, then at least one should recite the noon supererogatory prayers called *Awwābīn (*prayers of the oft-returning to God). In addition, perform the noon prayer at its new time, as this has been emphasized in the Noble Qur'ān; for it is

[41] That is, seventeen compulsory units and thirty-four supererogatory units (Translator's Note)

the noon prayer intended by the term 'middle prayer' in the Noble Qur'ān[42]

﴿حافِظوا عَلَى الصَّلَواتِ وَالصَّلاةِ الوُسطىٰ وَقوموا لِلَّهِ قانِتينَ﴾

﴿*ḥāfiẓū ʿalā ṣ-ṣalawāti wa-ṣ-ṣalāti l-wusṭā wa-qūmū li-llāhi qānitīna*﴾

﴿*Be watchful of your prayers, and [especially] the middle prayer*, and stand in obedience** to God*﴾

2. Regarding the Night Prayer, know that it is part of the compulsory acts for the believers and those who seek proximity with the Beloved, and there is no way around it! Nonetheless, it is astonishing for a person to have desires to reach the highest levels of

---

[42] Sūrat al-Baqarah, Verse 238.

* That is, the *ẓuhr* (noon) prayer, according to several traditions narrated from the Imams of the Prophet's Household, as well as many traditions narrated in the Sunnī sources (see *al-Tafsīr al-Burhān*, al-Ṭabarī's *Jāmiʿ al-Bayān*). According to other interpretations, the phrase 'the middle prayer' refers to the *ʿaṣr* (afternoon), *maghrib* (sunset) or *fajr* (dawn) prayer.

* Or 'stand humbly' (or 'prayerfully,' 'devoutly') before God.

perfection but to be inattentive to the performance of this supererogatory prayer! We have never seen or heard of any person reaching a station of perfection except through their steadfastness in the performance of the Night Prayer.

3. Reciting the Noble Qur'ān at the time of the Night Prayer is of extreme value to the wayfarer. It is this that will move him; instead, it will increase the speed of his journey. To "sing" the Noble Qur'ān takes one closer to God, unlike the forbidden singing, which takes man towards amusement and debauchery. Recite the Noble Qur'ān as much as you can during the night because it is the recitation of the Noble Qur'ān that is the intoxicant of the believer.

4. Ensure that you each recite the litanies and supplications that have individually been given to you as a practical instruction[43].

---

[43] This practical instruction was given to his students, so each of his students likely had a specific litany or supplication that he had to perform every day (Translator's Note)

Be constant in performing the *Yūnusiyah* prostration. That is, to recite the verse,

﴿أَن لَّا إِلَٰهَ إِلَّا أَنتَ سُبْحَانَكَ إِنِّي كُنتُ مِنَ الظَّالِمِينَ﴾

﴿*lā ʾilāha ʾillā ʾanta subḥānaka ʾinnī kuntu mina ẓ-ẓālimīnᵃ*﴾

﴿*There is no god except You! You are immaculate! I have indeed been among the wrongdoers!*﴾[44]

From five hundred to a thousand times while in prostration.

5. Ensure that you visit the mausoleum of Amīr al-Muʾminīn, Imām ʿAlī ﷺ every day, and, as much as possible, the grand masjids, i.e., Masjid of Kūfah and Masjid of Sahlah. The same goes for all other masjids. For a believer, a masjid is like a fish in water!

6. Always recite the *Tasbīḥ* of Sayyidah Fāṭimah al-Zahrāʾ ﷺ after every compulsory prayer, for it is considered to be one of the

---

[44] Sūrat al-Anbiyāʾ, Verse 87.

great litanies. Recite it at least once after every compulsory prayer.

7. One of the essential acts that must be done is to pray for the reappearance of the Imām of the Time عجل الله تعالى فرجه الشريف in the *qunūt* of the *Witr*[45] prayer, it must be done every day and with all supplications.

8. Another essential act is the recitation of the ziyāra, known as *Ziyāra Jāmiʿah al-Kabīrah,* on Fridays.

9. Ensure that your daily recitation of the Noble Qur'ān is not less than one part.

10. As much as possible, hasten to visit your virtuous friends; indeed, they are your companions on the path towards God's proximity and your aides at times of difficulty.

[45] That is the single unit of prayer that is prayed as the last part and unit of the Night Prayer (Translator's Note)

11. Ensure that you take the time to visit the graveyard once in a while (e.g., once a week), but do not do so at night.[46]

What do we have to do with this world? All it does is deceive and degrade us! It pulls us down from our station of honor and dignity! It is not worth being made the object of our desire, so leave it for its people!

Congratulations to those whose bodies are in this material world but whose hearts are flying toward the divine presence of God's splendor and grandeur!

Even though these individuals may be few, they possess the most and give the highest form of assistance.

You have heard what I have said, and I seek God's forgiveness.

(1357/1938)

---

[46] One of the benefits of this recommendation is that it reminds a person of death and his eventual resting place (Translator's Note).

www.ingramcontent.com/pod-product-compliance
Lightning Source LLC
Chambersburg PA
CBHW021337140626
46545CB00020B/2359
* 9 7 8 1 9 5 6 2 7 6 3 5 0 *